AI DISCOVERS 160,000 NEW VIRUSES

Future of Disease Research

The Power of Artificial Intelligence in Uncovering the Hidden Microbial World

J. Andy Peters

Table of Contents

Introduction

In the ever-evolving landscape of science and medicine, there are moments that redefine our understanding of the natural world. One such moment occurred when a team of researchers from Australia and China, armed with cutting-edge artificial intelligence, unlocked a treasure trove of over 160,000 previously unknown viruses. This breakthrough, achieved through the use of sophisticated machine learning algorithms, didn't just expand the boundaries of microbiology—it shattered them, opening a new frontier in disease research and medical science.

For years, viruses have been a source of fear, fascination, and frustration. They remain one of the most elusive, yet pervasive, threats to human health, causing everything from the common cold to pandemics like COVID-19. Despite decades of research, much of the viral world remained hidden, inaccessible to conventional scientific tools. But AI has changed all that. With its ability to analyze vast amounts of data and detect patterns beyond the capacity of the human eye, artificial intelligence has empowered researchers to uncover the hidden microbial world that has long remained just out of reach.

So why should this discovery matter to you, the reader? Because it represents a seismic shift in how we understand viruses, how we study them, and how we can one day combat them. The viruses discovered aren't just footnotes in a scientific paper—they could hold the key to preventing future outbreaks, developing new treatments, and potentially even curing diseases that have plagued humanity for centuries. In short, this is the future of healthcare, and it's happening now.

What makes this achievement even more remarkable is the international collaboration behind it. Researchers from the University of Sydney in Australia, working alongside their counterparts in China, brought together expertise from both continents to tackle one of the most ambitious projects in the history of virus discovery. Their combined efforts demonstrate the power of global collaboration and the shared commitment to pushing the boundaries of scientific knowledge. This is not just a scientific triumph; it's a testament to the potential of teamwork across borders, disciplines, and cultures.

As the study of viruses enters this new era, the role of artificial intelligence will only become more critical. The methods developed and refined through this research could change how scientists approach everything from vaccine development to virus surveillance. But perhaps more importantly, this breakthrough has opened the door to a future where we might better understand, and ultimately control, the microscopic agents that have shaped our history in ways we are only beginning to comprehend.

Chapter 1: Understanding the Invisible World of Viruses

Viruses are some of the most intricate and elusive organisms on Earth, existing at the edge of life itself. Unlike bacteria or fungi, viruses are not considered living organisms in the traditional sense because they cannot survive or reproduce on their own. Instead, they rely entirely on the cells of a host organism to replicate and propagate. Despite their simplicity in structure—essentially a protein shell encasing genetic material—viruses are incredibly complex in their behavior and impact.

Their role in global health is profound, as they are the culprits behind countless diseases that have affected humanity throughout history. From the devastating influenza pandemics to the ongoing challenges posed by HIV/AIDS, viral infections are responsible for significant morbidity and mortality worldwide. In recent decades, new viruses like SARS-CoV-2 have emerged with the power to change the course of entire societies, demonstrating the unpredictable and often catastrophic nature of viral outbreaks.

One of the most troubling aspects of viruses is their remarkable ability to mutate. This is not simply a byproduct of their replication process but a fundamental feature of their biology. As viruses infect cells and replicate, small errors can occur in their genetic code, leading to mutations. While many of these mutations are harmless, others can give the virus a survival advantage—whether it's resistance to antiviral drugs or the ability to spread more easily between hosts. This constant genetic evolution is why new strains of viruses, like the variants of SARS-CoV-2, continue to emerge, posing new challenges to public health.

The virus world is vast and constantly evolving. Yet, for all the scientific advancements made, much of it remains hidden, undetected by traditional methods of research. Only now, with the advent of artificial intelligence, are we beginning to peel back the layers of this complex world. What was once an invisible and seemingly impenetrable network of life is slowly being revealed, and in doing so, we are learning just how interconnected our health is with these microscopic entities that surround us.

The history of virus research is a tale of discovery, innovation, and persistence. For much of human history, viruses were nothing more than an invisible enemy. Scientists could observe the effects of viral diseases—ranging from the common cold to more deadly outbreaks like smallpox—but they had no understanding of what these afflictions were caused by. The first breakthrough came in the late 19th century, when scientists began to realize that these diseases were caused by agents smaller than bacteria, agents that couldn't be seen with the microscopes of the time.

The initial efforts to study viruses involved painstaking processes. Researchers would isolate the virus from infected individuals or animals, often through a series of trial and error, making it possible to observe the virus in its various stages of infection. They would then cultivate the virus by introducing it into living cells or animal tissues, hoping to identify the pattern of infection and the specific way the virus replicated. This was an incredibly slow process—requiring a deep understanding of cell biology, tissue culture techniques, and often, years of trial.

Classifying viruses was another daunting challenge. Unlike bacteria, which could be easily cultured and identified by their shape, size, and behavior, viruses required more complex methods. Early virologists relied heavily on the ability to observe the way viruses interacted with cells, watching under microscopes as the virus infected and hijacked the cellular machinery to replicate itself. But since viruses are too small to be seen under even the most powerful optical microscopes, scientists had to rely on indirect methods like electron microscopy or molecular biology techniques to detect their presence.

It wasn't until the mid-20th century that advances in technology, such as the invention of electron microscopes, began to make the process of observing and classifying viruses more feasible. This allowed virologists to see the structure of viruses for the first time—revealing their protein shells, their genetic material, and their sometimes intricate, crystalline formations. Yet even with these tools, the task remained immense, with researchers needing to sift through countless samples and classify them according to various criteria, such as shape, size, and type of genetic material.

This traditional approach to virus research, while groundbreaking at the time, was slow and labor-intensive. It took years, even decades, to catalog the viruses that had already been identified, and countless others remained beyond reach. The discovery of new viral species often felt like finding a needle in a haystack, requiring significant resources and time. In short, virus research was a labor of patience and precision—a painstaking effort that, while necessary, left many viral diseases still cloaked in mystery.

As we'll see, it is this very challenge that led to the need for a revolutionary change in the way viruses are discovered and understood—a shift that would come in the form of artificial intelligence.

Traditional virus research methods, while groundbreaking in their time, have inherent limitations that became increasingly apparent as the scope of viral diversity expanded. These techniques, which relied heavily on isolation, classification, and microscopic observation, proved to be slow, labor-intensive, and, most critically, limited in their ability to detect unknown viruses and fully understand their impact on human health.

One of the most glaring limitations was the dependency on culturing viruses in living cells or animal tissues. This process, while effective for studying some viruses, was not universally applicable. Many viruses do not thrive in laboratory conditions, making them difficult, if not impossible, to isolate using traditional methods. As a result, numerous viruses—particularly those that do not cause visible symptoms in hosts or that mutate rapidly—remained undetected and unstudied.

Moreover, traditional methods were often limited to the identification of viruses that were already known or that fit into pre-established categories. The complexity of viral genetics, coupled with the immense diversity of viruses in nature, meant that many remained elusive to researchers. When a new virus appeared, as with the recent emergence of viruses like Zika or SARS-CoV-2, the slow pace of traditional detection methods made it challenging to respond quickly or fully understand the virus's characteristics and potential health impact.

The inability to quickly identify and understand the behavior of these viruses often led to delayed responses to outbreaks, leaving healthcare systems scrambling to catch up. This slow reaction time was particularly evident in the early days of the

COVID-19 pandemic, where traditional research methods struggled to keep up with the virus's rapid mutation and spread. The lack of real-time insights into the virus's genetic makeup, its potential for mutation, and its interaction with different populations meant that health authorities were playing catch-up rather than proactively mitigating the crisis.

In addition, the limited capacity to detect unknown viruses meant that many potential threats to public health went unnoticed. In the past, many viruses could only be studied after they had caused significant disease outbreaks, making it difficult to predict or prevent future pandemics. This delayed response to emerging viruses posed a critical gap in global health preparedness.

These limitations are precisely why the recent breakthrough in AI-driven virus discovery is so important. For the first time, scientists now have the tools to analyze vast amounts of genomic data quickly and accurately, detecting viruses that were previously hidden from view. AI's ability to sift through enormous datasets and identify patterns in virus behavior offers the potential to revolutionize the way we study and respond to viral threats—giving us the capacity to understand and counter viruses before they become global health crises.

Chapter 2: Enter AI – The Game-Changer

Artificial Intelligence (AI) refers to the simulation of human intelligence in machines that are programmed to think, learn, and perform tasks that typically require human cognition. AI systems are designed to process large amounts of data, recognize patterns, make decisions, and improve their performance over time, all without direct human intervention. At its core, AI aims to mimic the ways humans think, solve problems, and make decisions, but with the added benefit of being able to process information at speeds and scales far beyond human capabilities.

There are several forms of AI, ranging from simple rule-based systems to more complex, self-learning algorithms. Broadly speaking, AI can be divided into two categories:

1. **Narrow AI (Weak AI)**: This is the most common form of AI in use today. Narrow AI refers to systems designed to perform a specific

task or set of tasks. Examples include facial recognition software, recommendation engines, or voice assistants like Siri and Alexa. These systems excel at their designated tasks but lack the broader capabilities of human intelligence.

2. **General AI (Strong AI)**: This type of AI is theoretical and has not yet been realized. General AI would possess the ability to understand, learn, and apply knowledge across a wide range of tasks, much like a human being. A machine with general AI would be able to reason, solve problems creatively, and make decisions in any area of expertise—tasks that current AI systems cannot do.

Within the realm of AI, one of the most significant and transformative subfields is **machine learning (ML)**. Machine learning is a method of data analysis that automates analytical model building. It is based on the idea that systems can learn from data, identify patterns, and make decisions with minimal human intervention. Unlike traditional programming, where developers write specific instructions for every action, machine learning enables computers to learn from examples and improve over time without being explicitly programmed to do so.

There are three primary types of machine learning:

1. **Supervised Learning**: In this approach, the machine is trained on a labeled dataset, meaning the input data comes with corresponding outputs. The algorithm learns to map inputs to outputs and makes predictions based on new, unseen data. Supervised learning is used in applications like spam email detection, medical diagnosis, and fraud detection.

2. **Unsupervised Learning**: Here, the machine is given data without explicit labels and must find patterns and structures on its own. This form of learning is particularly useful for clustering data into groups or identifying anomalies. It's often applied in customer

segmentation, market research, and image recognition.

3. **Reinforcement Learning**: This type of learning is inspired by behavioral psychology and involves training algorithms to make a series of decisions by rewarding or penalizing them based on the actions they take. Over time, the system learns to maximize rewards and minimize penalties, which makes reinforcement learning particularly useful in robotics, gaming, and autonomous vehicles.

Machine learning is at the heart of many recent breakthroughs, particularly in fields like virus research, where AI is used to analyze vast amounts of biological data, uncover hidden patterns, and make predictions about how viruses behave and evolve. By enabling machines to process and learn from data more efficiently than humans ever could, AI, particularly machine learning, is transforming the way we understand and combat viral diseases.

Artificial intelligence has already made a profound impact across a variety of scientific fields, revolutionizing the way researchers approach complex problems. In medicine, for example, AI is used to predict disease outbreaks, analyze medical images, and even assist in drug discovery. In astronomy, it has helped identify distant planets and map the universe with unprecedented detail. Similarly, in environmental science, AI is being applied to monitor climate change, predict natural disasters, and optimize renewable energy systems. In all these cases, AI's ability to process massive datasets and detect patterns has opened up new possibilities for understanding phenomena that were previously too complex or too vast for human researchers to tackle.

When it comes to virus discovery, AI's transformative potential has become even more apparent. For decades, virus research was limited by the capacity of traditional methods to isolate, identify, and categorize new viruses. AI has changed the game by enabling researchers to analyze viral data on a scale and speed that was unimaginable just a few years ago. Rather than painstakingly isolating individual viruses from infected samples, AI tools now allow scientists to sift through massive amounts of genetic data in a fraction of the time. This approach has not only sped up the discovery of new viruses but also allowed for the identification of viral species that had eluded detection through conventional methods.

At the heart of these advancements are cutting-edge machine learning algorithms, which have been specially designed to recognize complex patterns within vast datasets. One such tool is deep learning, a subset of machine learning that mimics the way the human brain processes information. Deep learning algorithms are particularly adept at analyzing genomic sequences and identifying viral signatures that might be overlooked by human researchers. These algorithms work by training on existing viral data, learning to detect subtle patterns and correlations that point to the presence of a virus, even in completely new or unknown strains.

Another powerful tool in the AI toolkit is natural language processing (NLP), which allows computers to analyze and interpret vast quantities of scientific literature and data in real-time. Researchers use NLP to scan thousands of articles, medical reports, and research papers to extract relevant information about emerging viruses and their potential impact on human health. This ability to rapidly process and synthesize information helps researchers stay ahead of the curve, identifying potential threats before they become global crises.

In addition to machine learning and NLP, AI has also enabled the creation of predictive models, which use historical data to forecast future trends in viral outbreaks. These models can simulate how a virus might spread across populations, taking into account factors like mutation rates, transmission methods, and environmental influences. By integrating AI into this predictive work, researchers are better equipped to prepare for and respond to emerging viral threats, potentially saving lives and mitigating the impact of future pandemics.

The combination of these advanced AI tools and techniques has completely changed the landscape of virus research, allowing scientists to uncover hidden viral species, track mutations with incredible precision, and respond to viral threats more swiftly than ever before. As AI continues to evolve, the possibilities for what it can achieve in the realm of disease research and prevention are truly limitless.

Chapter 3: The Groundbreaking Discovery of 160,000 New Viruses

The discovery of 160,000 new viruses was nothing short of a scientific breakthrough, and it was AI that made this massive leap in viral research possible. For years, scientists had been aware of the vast, unexplored microbial world—an ecosystem teeming with viruses that, while not necessarily harmful, could hold the key to new discoveries in medicine, genetics, and even the origins of life itself. However, finding these elusive viruses, particularly those that do not directly infect humans or that exist in environments hard to reach, posed a significant challenge for traditional methods. That's where artificial intelligence came in, transforming the process of virus discovery into something far more efficient, precise, and expansive.

The researchers, a collaborative team from Australia and China, used a combination of machine learning algorithms and sophisticated data analysis techniques to uncover a staggering number of previously unknown viral species. Instead of relying on conventional virus isolation and cultivation, they turned to a groundbreaking approach known as **metagenomics**, which allows scientists to sequence the DNA or RNA of entire ecosystems—like soil, water, or the human microbiome—without needing to isolate individual species first. This technique has been used in various fields, but it's the ability of AI to process and analyze the massive data sets produced by metagenomics that turned a challenging task into a feasible one.

Machine learning, a core aspect of AI, was the driving force behind this discovery. The researchers employed a series of advanced algorithms capable of handling enormous amounts of genetic data, identifying patterns and anomalies that would be invisible to the human eye. These machine learning models, trained on existing viral genomes, were able to "learn" the specific genetic markers of viruses and then apply this knowledge to identify similar sequences in the new data. By doing so, the AI systems could not only identify known viruses but also spot entirely new, previously unrecognized species. Essentially, the algorithms acted as a kind of "genetic detective," sifting through oceans of data to find viral sequences that didn't match any previously cataloged virus, signaling the presence of a new, undiscovered species.

This process was made possible through the use of **deep learning**—a subset of machine learning that mimics the neural networks of the human brain. Deep learning algorithms are particularly good at recognizing patterns in complex, unstructured data, making them perfect for tasks like virus discovery, where the data can be messy and non-linear. The more data these algorithms processed, the better they became at predicting and identifying viral sequences, improving with each iteration.

The significance of this discovery lies not only in the sheer number of new viruses identified but also in the potential these new viral species hold for future research. Some of these viruses could be harmless, existing silently in the environment, while others might hold the key to better understanding viral evolution or even potential therapies. What AI brought to the table was the ability to scale the search for these viral species in a way that was previously unimaginable, casting a much wider net and bringing back results that may have taken traditional methods decades to uncover.

The discovery of over 160,000 new viruses is an extraordinary leap in the world of scientific research, especially considering how many of these viruses were previously hidden from detection. To put the scale into perspective, before this breakthrough, researchers had identified a fraction of this number. The sheer magnitude of this discovery is not just a milestone in cataloging viruses; it fundamentally shifts our understanding of the viral world. With AI's help, these viruses, many of which exist in environments like soil, water, and even the human microbiome, were brought into focus—offering a glimpse into an entirely new realm of potential biological interactions that could have far-reaching consequences for medicine, health, and disease prevention.

The discovery also underscores the immense diversity of viruses, many of which belong to a class known as **RNA viruses**. RNA viruses are a specific type of virus that rely on ribonucleic acid (RNA) as their genetic material, rather than the more stable DNA found in many other organisms. These viruses are characterized by their ability to mutate rapidly, which allows them to adapt quickly to changing environments. This is one of the reasons why RNA viruses are often associated with some of the most significant global disease outbreaks, including the flu, HIV, and, more recently, COVID-19.

The significance of these newly discovered RNA viruses extends far beyond their cataloging. In the past, researchers had been limited in their understanding of RNA viruses due to the challenges in detecting them. With this breakthrough, the floodgates have been opened to study RNA viruses in a way that has never been possible before. These viruses could potentially hold the key to understanding new diseases, as well as new treatments or vaccines. Given their ability to mutate and cause pandemics, understanding RNA viruses on a deeper level is crucial to anticipating and preventing future outbreaks.

Moreover, many of these newly discovered viruses may not immediately pose a threat to human health, but they can offer valuable insights into viral behavior, gene flow, and interactions with their hosts. By examining the genetic material of these viruses, scientists can better understand how viruses evolve, how they spread, and how they might jump from animals to humans—an increasingly important concern as climate change and human encroachment on natural habitats bring us into closer contact with wildlife.

The AI-assisted discovery of these viruses also offers the possibility of more proactive approaches to global health. If we can better understand the full spectrum of viruses that exist in the world, we may be able to anticipate the emergence of new pathogens before they cause widespread disease. The hope is that by detecting viral species early, scientists can develop interventions that minimize their potential impact on human populations, rather than waiting for the next outbreak to occur.

In essence, this discovery not only expands the database of known viruses but also lays the groundwork for a new era of viral research. With these new tools and insights, the scientific community is better equipped to face the challenges of future viral outbreaks, including those that may arise unexpectedly. The implications for global disease prevention, healthcare, and even the development of antiviral treatments are enormous—this breakthrough could be the key to improving our ability to respond to viruses before they become global health crises.

Chapter 4: The Science Behind the Discovery

The technology that enabled the discovery of 160,000 new viruses is rooted in the powerful capabilities of **machine learning (ML)**, a subset of artificial intelligence that has the ability to analyze vast datasets and identify patterns that would be invisible to the human eye. Machine learning works by training algorithms on large volumes of data, allowing the system to "learn" from that data and improve its performance over time. In this case, the large datasets consisted of viral genetic sequences—an incredibly complex and massive pool of information that, without AI, would be nearly impossible to process manually.

At the heart of this discovery was **supervised learning**, one of the core techniques in machine learning. Supervised learning involves training an algorithm on labeled data, meaning the data has already been categorized in some way. For this study, the algorithm was fed known viral genetic sequences, which were labeled as belonging to particular virus families or species. By learning from these known examples, the machine could begin to recognize similar patterns in new, unclassified data. This allowed the system to classify and identify new viruses without the need for traditional isolation and observation methods.

Once the algorithm was trained, it was able to analyze **metagenomic data**, which is essentially genetic data gathered from environmental samples, such as soil, water, or even the human microbiome. In traditional virus discovery, this process would involve extracting and isolating viral samples, a painstaking and often fruitless task. But with AI, researchers were able to analyze this metagenomic data directly, without needing to culture individual viruses or look for obvious signs of infection. The machine learning algorithms sifted through this data, identifying patterns in the genetic sequences that indicated the presence of novel viruses.

The breakthrough came in the form of **unsupervised learning**, another technique within machine learning. Unsupervised learning does not rely on pre-labeled data. Instead, the algorithm is given raw data and asked to find structure or patterns on its own. This was crucial because many of the viruses discovered did not fit neatly into existing categories. Unsupervised learning algorithms were able to group similar genetic sequences together, identifying clusters of viruses that had never been seen before. Through this method, AI not only detected previously known viruses but also found entirely new species that had never been detected or classified.

The real magic of AI here was its ability to process and compare billions of data points, making connections that humans simply couldn't make on their own. The algorithms identified subtle genetic markers and trends across vast datasets, providing a clearer, more comprehensive picture of viral diversity. Where traditional methods would have taken years—if not decades—to achieve, AI was able to uncover in a matter of months.

Moreover, the use of **deep learning**, a more advanced form of machine learning, allowed the system to continuously refine its approach. Deep learning models, which are based on artificial neural networks that mimic the way the human brain processes information, were able to "understand" the complex relationships between different viral genomes. These networks can learn hierarchies of features, from the simplest to the most complex, enabling them to detect even the most minute variations in genetic material that could indicate a new virus.

In essence, AI's role in this discovery wasn't just in processing data—it was in transforming how that data was understood. By automating the process of data analysis, machine learning provided researchers with the ability to explore the viral landscape at an unprecedented scale, identifying viruses that might otherwise have remained hidden for years or even centuries. This technology doesn't just streamline the discovery process; it opens up entirely new avenues for research, allowing scientists to uncover viral diversity that could one day hold the key to preventing future pandemics or understanding the origins of complex diseases.

RNA viruses have long been among the most difficult to study due to their inherent characteristics. Unlike DNA viruses, which tend to be more stable, RNA viruses are highly prone to mutations. This genetic instability allows them to rapidly evolve, often leading to new strains that are resistant to treatments or immune responses. Viruses like HIV, influenza, and the SARS-CoV-2 coronavirus are all RNA-based, and their constant genetic shifts pose significant challenges for traditional methods of virus detection and classification. The difficulty in tracking these rapid mutations is compounded by the vast number of RNA viruses in nature, many of which infect organisms without causing obvious symptoms, leaving them undetected.

However, the discovery of 160,000 new viruses, including many RNA viruses, became possible due to the power of artificial intelligence. Traditional methods of virus discovery, which relied on isolating and culturing viruses in laboratory conditions, were not only time-consuming but also largely ineffective for RNA viruses that didn't easily replicate in lab environments. AI, on the other hand, is not limited by these constraints. By analyzing vast datasets of viral genetic sequences using advanced machine learning algorithms, AI can spot patterns and variations in RNA sequences that would be nearly impossible for human researchers to detect manually.

Machine learning models, particularly those using deep learning techniques, can process enormous amounts of genetic data at once. These algorithms were trained to recognize the subtle genetic signatures of RNA viruses—signatures that might not appear in viruses with stable, predictable genomes. For example, machine learning tools were able to detect small but significant genetic markers within RNA sequences, flagging them as potential viral candidates. What's more, AI could quickly compare these new sequences with previously identified viruses, helping researchers categorize them and distinguish between known and unknown species.

Moreover, AI's capacity for "unsupervised learning" allowed it to identify new, previously unknown viral strains. Rather than relying solely on pre-existing knowledge of viral families, unsupervised learning models could analyze genetic data without predefined labels, allowing the system to classify viruses based on patterns in the data itself. This meant that even viruses that didn't fit into familiar categories could still be detected and included in the analysis.

AI's ability to continuously learn and improve its predictions also meant that as more viral data became available, the system's accuracy and efficiency increased. Over time, the machine learning algorithms became more adept at identifying the complex mutations and unique genetic features of RNA viruses, which might have taken human researchers years to detect using traditional methods.

This breakthrough in RNA virus discovery is a testament to the power of AI in transforming scientific research. It not only allows researchers to uncover new viral species more quickly, but it also enables the study of RNA viruses on a scale never before possible, offering critical insights into their behavior, mutation rates, and potential to cause future outbreaks. With AI at the forefront, researchers now have a powerful tool to monitor and understand the rapidly evolving world of RNA viruses, giving us a better chance of staying ahead of future viral threats.

Chapter 5: Unveiling the Undiscovered Microbial World

The microbial world is far broader and more complex than we can perceive with the naked eye. Beneath the surface of our environment, in the soil, oceans, air, and even inside our bodies, lies a vast array of microorganisms, many of which we have only begun to understand. Viruses, in particular, represent one of the most enigmatic and poorly understood components of this world. For decades, scientists knew that viruses were everywhere, but the sheer scale and diversity of the viral landscape remained a mystery. Only a tiny fraction of viruses had been discovered through traditional methods, and many of those we did know about were the ones that had clear effects on human health. But the vast majority—those that exist in obscure environments, or that do not directly cause diseases in humans—remained undetected.

Artificial intelligence is now providing a window into this hidden world, dramatically expanding our ability to discover new viruses and understand their roles in ecosystems. Unlike traditional virus discovery, which relies on culturing and isolating specific viruses, AI allows for the analysis of environmental samples in their entirety, without the need to identify individual viruses upfront. This method, known as **metagenomics**, enables researchers to sequence the genetic material from entire ecosystems, giving them a comprehensive view of the microbial world. By using machine learning to analyze these genetic sequences, AI can spot patterns and identify viruses that would have otherwise remained invisible.

What makes AI so powerful in this context is its ability to process massive amounts of data—far more than any human researcher could manage manually. The algorithms can sift through millions of genetic sequences and detect even the faintest viral signatures, revealing hidden viruses that might otherwise be overlooked. This is especially important in environments that are difficult to access or study, such as deep-sea ecosystems or remote areas of the planet, where unique viruses may exist that have never before been identified.

The implications of this discovery are profound. By uncovering previously undetected viruses, AI opens up new avenues for scientific research in a number of fields. For one, understanding the full scope of viral diversity helps us better anticipate potential threats to human health. Many viruses that are harmless to humans might hold key insights into viral evolution or immunity. Furthermore, discovering new viruses in natural environments could lead to the identification of novel compounds or genes that have therapeutic potential. These insights could be crucial in developing new antiviral treatments, vaccines, or other medical interventions.

Beyond medicine, the discovery of hidden viruses is revolutionizing our understanding of ecosystems and ecological interactions. Viruses are not just agents of disease—they play a critical role in regulating populations of bacteria, fungi, and other microorganisms, maintaining the balance of ecosystems. By studying these viruses, researchers can gain insights into how ecosystems function and how they might respond to environmental changes, such as climate change or habitat destruction.

In short, the ability to detect hidden viruses using AI is unlocking a new era of scientific discovery. It is providing a deeper understanding of the microbial world and offering unprecedented opportunities to explore, protect, and potentially harness the power of the viruses that shape life on Earth. Through AI, we are not just uncovering more viruses—we are opening the door to a host of new possibilities for medicine, ecology, and beyond.

The discovery of 160,000 new viruses through AI not only represents a leap forward in our understanding of viral diversity but also carries profound long-term implications for human health. As researchers uncover these previously hidden viruses, the knowledge they gain could play a crucial role in predicting, preventing, and managing future disease outbreaks. Viruses, especially RNA viruses, evolve rapidly, and the ability to track these changes will be essential in staying one step ahead of potential pandemics. AI's capacity to analyze viral genetic data in real time, identify patterns in mutation, and predict how viruses might evolve opens up new avenues for anticipating the emergence of new viral strains before they pose a significant threat to public health.

Understanding the full extent of viral diversity is key to this. Many of the newly discovered viruses are likely to have a far-reaching impact on ecosystems that were previously unexplored or poorly understood. AI allows researchers to detect these viruses without the need for direct observation or isolation, which means that even viruses that don't directly infect humans—or that have mild or undetectable effects—can be studied. By cataloging viral genomes, AI helps build a more comprehensive picture of the viral landscape, which is crucial in identifying potential zoonotic threats, viruses that can jump from animals to humans.

Moreover, AI is transforming our understanding of viral mutation. The process of mutation is central to how viruses evolve and adapt. Through machine learning, researchers are not only able to identify existing mutations but also predict future changes in viral genomes. This predictive capability is invaluable for monitoring how viruses like influenza or SARS-CoV-2 might evolve in response to new treatments, vaccines, or environmental pressures. Understanding viral evolution through AI may eventually allow us to develop better vaccines and antiviral therapies, tailored to anticipated mutations before they even occur.

As AI continues to unravel the complexities of viral biology, we are moving toward a future where we can more effectively control, mitigate, and even prevent viral outbreaks. This newfound knowledge about viral diversity and mutation holds the potential to reshape how we approach infectious diseases, equipping scientists with the tools needed to tackle emerging health threats in real-time. The ability to predict viral behavior, track mutations, and understand the full scope of viral biodiversity could be the key to not only managing future pandemics but preventing them altogether.

Chapter 6: The Implications for Global Health

The practical implications of discovering 160,000 new viruses are immense, especially when it comes to global health and the prevention of future pandemics. The rapid pace at which new viral strains emerge—often unpredictably—has been a central concern in public health for decades. HIV, Ebola, SARS, Zika, and most recently, COVID-19, are just a few examples of viruses that have made the jump from animals or obscure environments to humans, often with devastating consequences. Traditionally, identifying and understanding these viruses has been a lengthy and resource-intensive process. However, the power of artificial intelligence is now providing a game-changing tool to not only discover new viruses more quickly but also to predict how they might evolve, giving scientists and public health officials a better chance to respond before an outbreak spirals out of control.

AI's ability to analyze vast amounts of viral genetic data from a wide range of sources—from environmental samples to human clinical data—allows researchers to identify new viral strains early on, often before they have the chance to spread significantly. This proactive detection means that we can monitor viral evolution in real-time, tracking mutations that could lead to more dangerous or contagious variants. By pinpointing emerging threats in their early stages, AI can help shape targeted containment strategies and public health responses, preventing a new virus from causing a full-scale epidemic or pandemic.

In terms of vaccine development, AI's impact is equally transformative. Historically, developing vaccines has been a slow, trial-and-error process. Once a virus is identified, researchers must isolate it, understand its structure, and then design a vaccine to counter it. With the sheer number of new viruses now being identified through AI, the potential for vaccines to be developed more quickly and efficiently is greater than ever. By analyzing the genetic sequences of newly discovered viruses, AI can help identify viral strains with the highest potential for human infection and rapid mutation. This can direct researchers' focus to those viruses that pose the greatest threat, allowing them to prioritize vaccine development and response efforts.

Additionally, AI can optimize the process of vaccine design by predicting how a virus might mutate and how these changes could affect its ability to infect humans or evade immunity. This predictive capability could lead to more effective, long-lasting vaccines that are able to protect against multiple viral strains or future mutations. By streamlining vaccine development and improving the accuracy of predictions about viral behavior, AI has the potential to save countless lives by making vaccines more responsive, efficient, and timely.

Ultimately, the integration of AI into viral research could redefine how we approach infectious disease prevention and treatment. By giving us a deeper understanding of viral evolution and enabling quicker responses to emerging threats, AI is helping to build a more resilient and proactive global health system, one that is better equipped to handle the challenges of the future.

The integration of AI into diagnostic tools has the potential to revolutionize the speed and accuracy with which we detect viral infections. Traditionally, diagnosing viral diseases has been a slow and sometimes imprecise process, often requiring time-consuming laboratory tests to isolate and identify the virus in question. In contrast, AI's ability to process vast amounts of complex viral data at incredible speed allows for the development of diagnostic tools that can provide near-instantaneous results, often with a higher degree of accuracy than conventional methods.

One of the key ways AI enhances diagnostic tools is by enabling **pattern recognition**. AI algorithms can be trained on large datasets of viral genetic sequences, as well as the symptoms and outcomes associated with specific infections. Once trained, these algorithms can analyze new data—whether it's a blood sample, a swab, or genetic information—and quickly identify the presence of specific viral strains. This is particularly valuable in cases where the virus is novel, or when symptoms are subtle or overlap with other diseases. With AI, diagnostics can go beyond merely identifying known pathogens; they can detect previously unrecognized mutations, predict how a virus is likely to evolve, and identify strains that may not yet be included in traditional testing protocols.

Furthermore, AI can help **optimize diagnostic accuracy** by reducing human error, which can sometimes occur when interpreting complex genetic or viral data. Machine learning models can sift through massive amounts of data more quickly than a human ever could, and in some cases, they can spot subtle patterns or genetic variations that might be missed by traditional diagnostic methods.

This is especially important in viral diseases that mutate quickly, where early detection of new strains is crucial for containment and treatment.

Overall, AI-driven diagnostics could drastically reduce the time it takes to identify viral infections, making it possible to begin treatment or containment efforts almost immediately. This could be particularly valuable during an outbreak or in areas with limited access to medical resources, where fast and accurate diagnostic tools are often in short supply.

Chapter 7: Ethical Concerns and Risks

As artificial intelligence becomes an increasingly integral part of scientific research, especially in fields like virus discovery, it is essential to address the ethical concerns and potential risks that accompany its use. While AI holds immense promise for advancing our understanding of the microbial world and improving global health, it also raises important questions about control, privacy, and the potential for misuse.

One of the primary ethical concerns is **control**—specifically, who owns and controls the AI systems and the data they process. AI-driven research relies on vast datasets, often containing sensitive information, such as genetic sequences from human populations or even private health data. The question of who has access to these datasets and who benefits from the resulting discoveries is crucial. There is a need for transparency in how data is collected, used, and shared, as well as clear guidelines to ensure that AI research benefits society at large rather than a select few.

Privacy is another major concern, particularly when AI is used to analyze medical data. While AI can help diagnose diseases and track viral mutations, the use of personal health information—often extracted from electronic health records, genetic databases, or epidemiological surveys—must be done with strict adherence to privacy regulations like GDPR (General Data Protection Regulation) or HIPAA (Health Insurance Portability and Accountability Act). The risks of data breaches or unauthorized access to sensitive health information can have serious consequences, both for individuals and for public trust in scientific research.

Moreover, the **potential for misuse** of AI in virus discovery raises alarms. If AI tools are not properly regulated or are used irresponsibly, there is the possibility of creating or spreading harmful viruses, either intentionally or unintentionally. While AI can help researchers identify new viruses, there are risks if these discoveries fall into the wrong hands. For example, AI-powered research could potentially accelerate bioterrorism efforts, enabling malicious actors to create or engineer viruses for harmful purposes. This highlights the need for ethical frameworks and international oversight to ensure that AI is used safely and responsibly.

In addition to these concerns, there are the **unintended consequences** of relying too heavily on AI in virus discovery. While AI can process vast amounts of data with incredible speed and accuracy, it is not infallible. Algorithms can be prone to errors, particularly when they are trained on incomplete or biased datasets. There is a risk of **misidentification**—AI might wrongly classify a virus or overlook a potentially dangerous mutation, leading to inaccurate conclusions. In some cases, AI may also overfit to the data, identifying patterns that are not actually significant or that don't translate well into real-world situations.

There is also the danger of **overreliance** on technology. While AI is a powerful tool, it should not replace human expertise and critical thinking. Relying solely on AI to interpret viral data could lead to a situation where researchers become too dependent on the system, neglecting to question or challenge the findings. This could stifle creativity, limit alternative explanations, and ultimately result in flawed conclusions. As with all scientific endeavors, AI should be viewed as a complement to, not a substitute for, human judgment.

Ultimately, as AI continues to shape the future of virus discovery and global health, it is crucial to maintain a balance between innovation and caution. Ethical oversight, transparency, and a commitment to using AI for the greater good will help ensure that its potential is harnessed in ways that benefit humanity, rather than inadvertently creating new risks or inequalities.

As AI continues to make its mark across scientific fields, including virus discovery and healthcare, the need for robust **regulation and oversight** has never been more critical. While AI's potential to accelerate research, improve diagnostics, and predict viral evolution is undeniable, it also brings with it a set of challenges that require careful management to ensure that the technology is used responsibly and ethically.

One of the primary reasons for regulation is to ensure **accuracy and reliability** in AI-driven research. AI algorithms are only as good as the data they are trained on, and if the data is flawed, biased, or incomplete, the results can be misleading. In the context of virus discovery, for example, incorrect identifications or misinterpretations of viral data could lead to false conclusions, which might hinder medical efforts or even cause harm. To prevent such errors, there needs to be oversight from regulatory bodies to verify the accuracy of AI models and the data they are based on. This includes setting standards for data quality, ensuring diversity in datasets to prevent biases, and conducting regular audits of AI systems used in scientific research.

Moreover, **ethics** plays a key role in the regulation of AI in science. The ability of AI to process vast amounts of personal and sensitive data, such as genetic sequences and medical histories, raises serious concerns about privacy and consent. Strict guidelines are necessary to ensure that individuals' rights are protected, and that their data is used in ways that are transparent, consensual, and secure. This is especially important when dealing with genomic data, where privacy breaches could have lifelong consequences for individuals.

Accountability is another area where regulation is essential. As AI systems become more autonomous in making decisions—such as identifying new viruses or determining potential treatments—questions about accountability will inevitably arise. Who is responsible if an AI system makes an error that leads to a misdiagnosis or a flawed research conclusion? Governments and scientific bodies must establish clear frameworks for determining liability and ensuring that researchers and institutions using AI are held accountable for the outcomes of their work.

Finally, there is the issue of **unintended consequences**. AI systems are designed to optimize for specific goals, but they do so in ways that might not always align with broader ethical or societal considerations. For example, the overreliance on AI in virus discovery might lead to a lack of human oversight, where critical insights or interpretations are overlooked because AI is treated as infallible. AI might also inadvertently prioritize certain viruses or data points, leading to skewed research outcomes or missed opportunities. Regulatory frameworks should ensure that human judgment and oversight remain integral to the process, preventing overdependence on technology.

The complexity and rapid evolution of AI technology necessitate a proactive approach to regulation. Scientific and governmental organizations must work together to create comprehensive guidelines that address these issues and ensure that AI is used in ways that maximize its benefits while minimizing its risks. Clear standards for transparency, accuracy, privacy protection, and accountability are essential for fostering trust in AI-powered research and ensuring that its impact is positive, equitable, and ethically sound.

Chapter 8: The Future of AI and Virus Discovery

The role of artificial intelligence in virus research is only in its infancy, and the future holds immense promise for further breakthroughs and applications that will significantly enhance our understanding of the microbial world. As AI systems evolve, they will continue to play a pivotal role in unlocking new layers of complexity in viral biology and their interactions with host organisms. This synergy between AI and traditional scientific methods will likely lead to rapid advances in areas such as viral evolution, vaccine development, and even the detection of emerging diseases.

One area where AI will undoubtedly make a significant impact is in **predictive modeling**. With the ability to process vast amounts of genomic, environmental, and epidemiological data, AI can predict how viruses might evolve, spread, or interact with different populations. This could enable scientists to anticipate potential outbreaks, identify high-risk regions, and even develop strategies for controlling viral transmission before it becomes a global threat. AI's ability to simulate viral mutation and predict changes in viral behavior could, for instance, help researchers design vaccines that are more adaptive to future strains, rather than being reactive to current ones.

AI will also continue to **augment human researchers** rather than replace them. While AI can sift through enormous datasets and identify patterns that may not be immediately obvious to human scientists, it is the human element that provides the context and expertise to interpret these findings. AI can assist in hypothesis generation, streamline repetitive tasks like data entry or sequence analysis, and offer insights that may otherwise go unnoticed. However, the final interpretation of AI's findings—particularly in complex areas like virus-host interactions or the potential implications of newly discovered viruses—will still require human creativity, expertise, and ethical consideration.

In the future, we may also see more **collaborative platforms** where AI works alongside scientists from different disciplines, integrating data from fields such as genomics, epidemiology, environmental science, and public health. By combining the strengths of AI with the deep understanding of virus biology and the practical experience of human researchers, the potential for cross-disciplinary breakthroughs becomes even greater. For instance, AI could integrate viral genomic data with climate models, predicting how environmental changes or shifts in human behavior might affect the emergence or spread of new viruses.

Ultimately, the collaboration between AI and human researchers represents the most promising path forward. AI's ability to handle vast amounts of data, identify hidden patterns, and make predictions will provide invaluable tools for scientists. Yet, it will be human ingenuity and ethical judgment that will steer this powerful technology toward its most beneficial uses. Together, AI and researchers will not only deepen our understanding of the microbial world but also pave the way for a healthier, more resilient future.

Beyond virus discovery, the potential for AI to transform global health is vast, spanning numerous areas of medical research, patient care, and public health management. As AI continues to evolve, its applications are poised to revolutionize the way we diagnose, treat, and prevent diseases, leading to more efficient, accurate, and personalized healthcare solutions. Here are a few key areas where AI could make a significant impact:

1. Personalized Medicine

One of the most promising applications of AI in healthcare is **personalized medicine**. By analyzing vast amounts of patient data, including genetic information, medical histories, lifestyle factors, and even real-time health data, AI can help tailor treatments to individual patients. This could involve predicting how patients will respond to certain medications, identifying potential risks for specific conditions, and recommending the most effective treatment plans. The ability to deliver highly customized care could improve outcomes and reduce side effects, ensuring that patients receive the best possible care based on their unique biological makeup.

2. Early Disease Detection

AI has the potential to dramatically improve **early disease detection**, enabling healthcare providers to identify conditions before they become life-threatening. By analyzing medical imaging, lab results, and patient records, AI systems can help detect early signs of cancer, heart disease, neurodegenerative disorders, and other conditions that might otherwise go unnoticed in their early stages. AI's ability to analyze patterns in complex datasets enables it to spot abnormalities that may be too subtle for human clinicians to detect, leading to earlier, more accurate diagnoses and better chances for successful treatment.

3. Predictive Modeling for Epidemics

AI's ability to process vast amounts of real-time data makes it invaluable in **predicting and managing epidemics**. By analyzing trends in health data, climate, population movement, and other factors, AI can identify early warning signs of disease outbreaks and predict how they might spread. For example, AI could help track the movement of infectious diseases like Ebola, Zika, or even the flu, and predict where future outbreaks are most likely to occur. This predictive power can help governments and health organizations take preventive measures more quickly, such as stockpiling medications, setting up quarantine zones, or launching vaccination campaigns before an outbreak escalates.

4. Drug Discovery and Vaccine Development

AI is already making waves in **drug discovery** and **vaccine development**, and its potential in these areas is immense. By analyzing vast datasets of chemical compounds, genetic data, and clinical trial results, AI systems can help identify promising new drug candidates faster and more accurately than traditional methods. This could shorten the time it takes to develop new treatments for diseases, from cancer to autoimmune disorders, and allow for more targeted therapies. In the case of vaccines, AI can be used to model how viruses mutate and predict which strains are most likely to cause future outbreaks, aiding in the development of vaccines that are more effective and longer-lasting.

5. Mental Health and Wellbeing

AI's role in **mental health** is another area with enormous potential. By analyzing patterns in speech, behavior, and physiological data, AI could help identify early signs of mental health conditions like depression, anxiety, and PTSD. Through natural language processing and emotion-sensing technology, AI systems could provide insights into patients' emotional states, offering early interventions or recommending therapeutic strategies tailored to the individual's needs. Additionally, AI-driven applications such as virtual therapists or chatbots could provide accessible, affordable mental health support, especially in underserved or remote areas where traditional mental health services are scarce.

6. Healthcare Accessibility and Efficiency

AI can also help improve **healthcare accessibility** and **efficiency**, especially in underserved regions. AI-powered telemedicine platforms can connect patients in remote areas with healthcare providers, allowing for virtual consultations, diagnoses, and follow-up care. AI algorithms can triage symptoms, recommend treatments, and even monitor patient progress remotely, reducing the need for in-person visits and making healthcare more accessible to those in rural or impoverished areas. Moreover, AI can streamline administrative tasks within hospitals and clinics, reducing wait times, minimizing human error, and allowing healthcare professionals to focus more on patient care.

7. Chronic Disease Management

Managing chronic diseases like diabetes, hypertension, and asthma requires constant monitoring and personalized care. AI-powered systems can help patients track their conditions in real time, offering insights and recommendations based on data from wearable devices, blood tests, and daily health logs. By using predictive analytics, AI can alert patients and healthcare providers to potential complications before they arise, enabling earlier interventions and better long-term outcomes. This proactive approach to chronic disease management could significantly improve the quality of life for millions of patients around the world.

8. Healthcare Inequality

AI has the potential to **reduce healthcare inequality** by making quality care more accessible and affordable, particularly in developing countries or low-income regions. AI-driven diagnostic tools, telemedicine, and mobile health applications can provide life-saving services to populations that would otherwise have limited access to healthcare. In addition, AI can be used to identify gaps in healthcare provision, track health disparities, and guide policy decisions to improve the distribution of resources and healthcare services.

In the coming decades, AI will continue to be a driving force in shaping the future of global health. Its ability to analyze large datasets, predict disease trends, and assist in treatment personalization will create more efficient, effective, and equitable healthcare systems. The promise of AI lies not just in its technical capabilities, but in its potential to create a healthier world by improving how we prevent, diagnose, and treat diseases across the globe.

Conclusion

The discovery of 160,000 new viruses, largely made possible by artificial intelligence, marks a monumental shift in our approach to scientific research. For centuries, viruses were an invisible force, their diversity and complexity largely hidden from our understanding. Now, thanks to AI, researchers have opened a new chapter in virus discovery, one where the scope of microbial life is far more expansive than we ever imagined. This breakthrough not only expands the boundaries of virology but also provides us with the tools to predict, track, and prevent viral outbreaks with unprecedented accuracy.

As we stand on the brink of this new era in scientific exploration, it's crucial to remember that the power of AI comes with a profound responsibility. The ethical use of AI—ensuring transparency, accountability, and equity—will be essential as we continue to push the boundaries of research. The potential for AI to misidentify viruses, over-rely on automated systems, or compromise sensitive data must be carefully managed. With proper oversight, AI has the power to revolutionize not just virus discovery but medicine, public health, and beyond.

Looking ahead, the future of virus research and healthcare is poised to benefit from AI-driven innovations that will shape a more informed, proactive approach to global health. By combining the immense computational power of AI with the insights of human researchers, we have the opportunity to address the challenges of today and tomorrow, from emerging pandemics to the ongoing pursuit of more effective treatments. As we embrace these advancements, we stand on the threshold of a future where science is more accessible, disease prevention is more effective, and healthcare is more personalized. The promise of AI is not just in the discoveries we've made so far, but in the new possibilities it will unlock for generations to come.